The U.S.'s Second Independence Day: Juneteenth

# Dr. Mike Eric Martin

# The U.S.'s Second Independence Day: Juneteenth

Copyright © 2024 Dr. Mike Eric Martin

All rights reserved.

ISBN: **9798345951675**

# The U.S.'s Second Independence Day: Juneteenth

## DEDICATION

I dedicate this book to my ancestors, whose shoulders I stand on. I am in awe of the conditions you endured and your resilience. You did not waver in your pursuit of equality, and because you stood firm, I am here today. Our society has come far, but we still have much work to be done. Devine Energy surrounds me, and I receive it with love.

# The U.S.'s Second Independence Day: Juneteenth

## CONTENT

Acknowledgment

Preface     vii

1. Introduction     10
2. The Road to Freedom     12
3. Slavery in the United States     15
4. The Complexities of Emancipation     17
5. The First Juneteenth Celebration     20
6. Juneteenth Traditions     25
7. The Evolution of Juneteenth     27
8. The Importance of Juneteenth Today     29
9. How Children Can Celebrate Juneteenth and Learn     32
10. A Message of Hope and Unity     35
11. Juneteenth Flag     37
12. The Role of Education in Preserving Juneteenth's Legacy     39
13. Juneteenth and the Arts     41
14. Future of Juneteenth     44
15. Economic Impact of Juneteenth     46
16. Juneteenth in the Global Context     48
17. Juneteenth in Popular Culture     50
18. Juneteenth and Political Activism     51
19. Chapter Juneteenth and the Church     53
20. Juneteenth Personal Stories     55
21. In Closing     59
22. Glossary     61
23. References     63

# The U.S.'s Second Independence Day: Juneteenth

# The U.S.'s Second Independence Day: Juneteenth

## ACKNOWLEDGMENTS

I would like to thank God, for planting the seed of inspiration to write this book on Juneteenth. Starting this journey and completing this project has been one of the many highlights of my year.

Dr. Byrian Ramsey, thank you for being my biggest supporter as I took time out of our lives for this project. Writing this book has been taxing and time-consuming, but your unwavering support has been invaluable even as it took longer than expected.

I also thank John L. Jolly for your invaluable help in fine-tuning this manuscript. Your editorial insights have helped shape this work into the best it could be.

# The U.S.'s Second Independence Day: Juneteenth

## Preface

The U.S.'s Second Independence Day: Juneteenth provides a strong foundation for introducing Juneteenth and its historical significance. It covers much important ground, tracing the history of Juneteenth celebrations from their beginnings to their recognition as a federal holiday. It delves into the complexities surrounding the Emancipation Proclamation and Abraham Lincoln's thoughts during that time. It dives into the importance of teaching all aspects of American history, especially those related to slavery and racism.

Juneteenth is a special day in June when many Americans celebrate the end of slavery. But did you know that other countries also remember the history of slavery in their ways? They hold different kinds of celebrations to acknowledge their roles in a time when people were taken from Africa and forced into slavery.

Even today, some people try to cover up parts of American history, pretending that the terrible things that happened during slavery weren't so bad. But the truth is, the United States has not done enough to make up for the wrongs of the past. Many ancestors suffered, treated as less than human, and our country still has work to do to bring peace and justice to their memories.

In this book, you'll learn about what led to the creation of Juneteenth and why it's such an important holiday. We'll explore the history of slavery in America and understand why Juneteenth is more than just a celebration, it reminds everyone of freedom and equality. Through this story, we hope to encourage children to ask questions, learn about

# The U.S.'s Second Independence Day: Juneteenth

their history, and feel uplifted by the message of Juneteenth.

Many numerous titles fall under the celebration of Juneteenth. This is a luxury list of examples of Juneteenth titles:

- Freedom Day
- Liberation Day
- Emancipation Day
- Juneteenth Jubilee
- Day of Freedom
- Heritage Day
- Juneteenth Independence Day
- Freedom and Unity Day
- Day of Resilience
- Liberty Day
- Day of Emancipation and Reflection
- Day of Justice
- National Day of Remembrance
- Day of African American Freedom
- Day of Reflection and Renewal
- Emancipation and Remembrance Day
- Juneteenth Freedom Festival
- Unity and Freedom Day
- Day of Honor and Memory
- Day of Triumph
- Slavery Remembrance Day

# The U.S.'s Second Independence Day: Juneteenth

# The U.S.'s Second Independence Day: Juneteenth

# The U.S.'s Second Independence Day: Juneteenth

## Chapter 1: Introduction to Juneteenth

On July 4, 1776, thirteen North American colonies declared their independence from Great Britain. However, two and a half years after President Abraham Lincoln signed the Emancipation Proclamation, which stated that all enslaved people were free, many in Galveston, Texas, remained in bondage. Around 250,000 enslaved people in Texas were unaware that they had been freed because the news had not reached them.[1] It wasn't until June 19, 1865, when Union General Gordon Granger and his troops arrived in Galveston that the enslaved residents finally learned they were free. They had lived under the brutal conditions of slavery for years, not knowing that it had officially ended.

What Americans need to understand is that Juneteenth is now a national holiday that marks the beginning of healing from this nation's original sin—244 years of slavery. In addition to those years, the people of Galveston endured an extra two and a half years of enslavement due to the delay in enforcing the Emancipation Proclamation. Juneteenth represents freedom and independence for all Americans and is a step toward the ideals of equality and liberty we strive for today.

For many years, Juneteenth was celebrated mostly in Texas, where communities held annual events to commemorate their newfound freedom. It wasn't until recent years that the rest of the country began to understand

---

[1] The President of the United States of America. (2024). Title 3--The President: Juneteenth Day of Observance, 2024. Washington, DC: Federal Information & News Dispatch, LLC. Retrieved from ProQuest Central: https://www.proquest.com/reports/title-3-president-juneteenth-day-observance-2024/docview/3071120891/se-2

# The U.S.'s Second Independence Day: Juneteenth

the importance of this celebration. On June 19, 2021, President Joe Biden officially declared Juneteenth a federal holiday, recognizing its significance in the evolution of American democracy.

Here's something to think about: Juneteenth opened the door for all Americans to have the right to vote, have a voice, dream, and pursue those dreams. It paved the way for everyone to express their freedom of speech without fear of retaliation. Juneteenth symbolizes the possibility for people of all racial backgrounds to work side by side, attend the same church, enjoy sporting events together, and marry the ones they love.

General Order No. 3 secured the Union Army's authority over Texas. The order stated the following:

The people of Texas are informed that, by a proclamation from the Executive of the United States, 'all slaves are free.' This involves an absolute equality of personal rights and rights of property between former masters and slaves, and the connection heretofore existing between them becomes that between employer and hired labor. The freedmen are advised to remain quietly at their present homes and work for wages. They are informed that they will not be allowed to collect at military posts and that they will not be supported in idleness either there or elsewhere.[2]

---

[2] Library of Congress. (n.d.). *Today in history - June 19.* https://www.loc.gov/item/today-in-history/june-19/

# The U.S.'s Second Independence Day: Juneteenth

## Chapter 2: The Road to Freedom

### The Transatlantic Slave Trade

The Transatlantic Slave Trade was a brutal system that forcibly removed millions of Africans from their homeland and transported them across the Atlantic Ocean to North America. Liverpool, England, became one of the key hubs of the Transatlantic Slave Trade, especially in the 18th century, playing a major role in transporting significant numbers of enslaved Africans across the Atlantic.[3] The trade connected Africa, America, and Europe in a triangular route, with major ports like Quidah, Benin, and Charleston, South Carolina serving as critical points.

The practice of slavery in the Americas lasted from the 16th to the 19th centuries, fueled by the labor needs of the colonial powers.[4] Between 10 to 12 million Africans were forcibly transported to North America during this period.[5] Enslaved Africans were often captured violently and sold into slavery by both European traders and complicit African leaders. They were packed into ships under inhumane conditions, enduring the horrors of the Middle Passage.

Once in America, enslaved Africans were treated as property and forced to work under brutal conditions on plantations, in mines, and in households. Families were torn apart, and generations were born into slavery without

---

[3] Edrich, P. (2023, August 22). *City coming to terms with its vital role in the slave trade: Liverpool legacy's as 'capital of transatlantic slave trade' remembered in series of events for Slavery Remembrance Day*. Liverpool Echo. Available from file:///C:/Users/echoa/Downloads/At_Home_in_the_World%E2%80%9D_Materi.pdf.

[4] Shobowale, S. (2022, August 17). *Globes shining light on the transatlantic slave trade: Artworks form a trail around the city as a reminder of our history*. Leicester Mercury, 18.
https://www.proquest.com/docview/2703043768?accountid=206742&sourcetype=Newspapers

[5] Ibid

# The U.S.'s Second Independence Day: Juneteenth

hope of freedom. Despite these circumstances, the resilience of enslaved people laid the foundation for the eventual fight for freedom.

The United States officially abolished the international slave trade in 1808, yet illegal trading continued for years afterward.[6] The Clotilda, the last known slave ship, carried 110 smuggled Africans to Alabama in 1860, and its survivors founded Africatown, creating a home away from home.[7]

While it is important to acknowledge that some Africans participated in the slave trade, there were significant differences in how enslaved people were treated within Africa versus in the Americas. Internal slaves in Africa were often incorporated into the families and communities where they lived, whereas enslaved people in the Americas faced some of the worst conditions imaginable.[8]

Understanding the Transatlantic Slave Trade is essential for grasping the significance of the Emancipation Proclamation and the eventual liberation of enslaved people in the United States. This history is central to the meaning of Juneteenth, a celebration of hope, perseverance, and the ongoing struggle for equality.

---

[6] Howard-Hassmann, R. E. (2022). Should the USA offer reparations to Africa for the transatlantic slave trade? *Society*, 59(3), 339–348. https://doi.org/10.1007/s12115-022-00682-3

[7] MSN. (n.d.). *The last known intact US slave ship is too broken and should stay underwater, a report recommends.* https://www.msn.com/en-us/the-last-known-intact-us-slave-ship-is-too-broken-and-should-stay-underwater-a-report-recommends/ar-AA1oxyYE

Howard-Hassmann, R. E. (2022). Should the USA offer reparations to Africa for the transatlantic slave trade? *Society*, 59(3), 339–348. https://doi.org/10.1007/s12115-022-00682-3

# The U.S.'s Second Independence Day: Juneteenth

## A Lasting Impact

The legacy of the Transatlantic Slave Trade is not just a chapter in history books but a profound reality that continues to affect descendants of enslaved Africans. The trauma and loss experienced by those enslaved have left deep scars on generations. The monuments and symbols of this dark past, such as Confederate statues, serve as constant reminders of the suffering and injustice that Black Americans have endured.

These symbols of oppression are a painful reminder of a time when Black people were considered three-fifths of a person under Article I, Section 2 of the U.S. Constitution.[9] The presence of these monuments in public spaces can be a source of pain for those who descend from the enslaved, as they glorify individuals who fought to uphold a system of brutal oppression.

As we reflect on the road to freedom, it's crucial to understand why there is a call for the removal of these monuments. It's not about erasing history but about healing and moving forward. Acknowledging the past, learning from it, and taking down symbols of hate are steps toward a future where freedom, equality, and justice prevail.

---

[9] Batchis, S. (2023, July 23). *History of racism must be taught: The United States was built on slavery. Yet, in many U.S. history courses, slavery is barely discussed. Philadelphia Inquirer*, E.1. https://www.proquest.com/docview/2840737224?accountid=206742&sourcetype=Newspapers

# The U.S.'s Second Independence Day: Juneteenth

## Chapter 3: Slavery in the United States

Recently, many groups have fought to remove certain parts of history from schools. However, all history should be taught so that students can understand the full story of their country. We need to ask ourselves why some people are so determined to erase the foundation that made the United States what it is today. Across the country, especially in the southern states, legislation is being pushed to ban books and limit what is taught in schools.[10] Some individuals believe that certain histories are too uncomfortable and could cause distress in students.[11] But the truth is, all American history—including the difficult and painful parts—should be taught everywhere: in public and private schools, neighborhood libraries, Sunday school rooms, community centers, family gatherings, sports fields, and even in courtrooms.

Some parents argue that teaching about the darker parts of history, like slavery, might make "white students feel bad about being white." But why should we whitewash the brains of our children? It's up to the gatekeepers—teachers, parents, and community leaders—to ensure that important information like African American history is taught fully. This includes the good, the bad, and the ugly sides of history. History isn't just for those who look like

---

[10] Batchis, S. (2023, July 23). *History of racism must be taught: The United States was built on slavery. Yet, in many U.S. history courses, slavery is barely discussed. Philadelphia Inquirer,* E.1. https://www.proquest.com/docview/2840737224?accountid=206742&sourcetype=Newspapers

[11] Juneteenth offers new ways to teach about slavery, black perseverance, and American history (2024). Pittsburgh: Real Times, Inc. Retrieved from https://www.proquest.com/blogs-podcasts-websites/juneteenth-offers-new-ways-teach-about-slavery/docview/3075481170/se-2

# The U.S.'s Second Independence Day: Juneteenth

the people in the stories, it's for everyone. Information is power, and everyone deserves to be informed.

Maybe this strikes a nerve: "Information is power." Some fear that if everyone knows the truth, there will be retaliation. But we are not here to repeat the past; we are here to learn from it and grow. The United States was built on the blood, sweat, and tears of enslaved people. Many White Americans still benefit from the wealth created by that system of racism, and it's time we all face that reality.

This chapter isn't about making anyone feel bad; it's about documenting the facts as they were. The United States needs to make up for the promises made to Black ancestors—promises that were broken. It's time to stop whitewashing history for political agendas and start teaching the truth so we can build a better future for everyone.

# The U.S.'s Second Independence Day: Juneteenth

## Chapter 4: The Complexities of Emancipation

As history tells us, the end of slavery in the United States began when President Abraham Lincoln signed the Emancipation Proclamation in 1863. This crucial document declared that all enslaved people in the Confederate states were free. However, history also reveals that Lincoln had moments of doubt about Emancipation.[12]

At one point, Lincoln considered renouncing the Emancipation if Confederate President Jefferson Davis agreed to return to the Union.[13] Lincoln also expected the Supreme Court to rule against emancipation if the Confederacy surrendered.[14] But the Civil War dragged on longer than anyone expected, and no such agreement was reached. With so many lives lost Emancipation remained a moral victory, a token prize in the ongoing conflict.

Since Jefferson Davis refused to rejoin the Union and stood firm on the Confederacy's independence, we'll never truly know what Lincoln might have done if the situation had turned out differently. But what we do know is that the Emancipation Proclamation of 1863 ultimately declared freedom for all enslaved people. And that is something we can celebrate, regardless of the underlying uncertainties.

---

[12] Schwartz, B. (2015). The Emancipation Proclamation: Lincoln's many second thoughts. *Society, 52*(6), 590–603. https://doi.org/10.1007/s12115-015-9954-7.

[13] Ibid
[14] Ibid

# The U.S.'s Second Independence Day: Juneteenth

## Lincoln's Struggles and the Delayed Freedom of Enslaved Texans

President Lincoln's journey toward issuing the Emancipation Proclamation was not straightforward. His hands were often tied by the political realities of his time. Lincoln opposed slavery as a cruel system, but he was also cautious about pushing too hard for Black equality, fearing it would alienate white moderates whose support he needed to keep the Union together.

Even after the Emancipation Proclamation was issued, the fear among some White Americans that Black people would seek vengeance for the centuries of injustice they endured remained strong. This fear, coupled with political motivations, contributed to the delay in freeing enslaved people in Texas. Despite the proclamation being signed in 1863, it took more than two years for the news to reach Texas.

One significant factor in this delay was the lack of Union troops in the South, especially in remote areas like Texas. The Union's military presence was thin, making it difficult to enforce the new law.[15] To address this, the Union allowed Black men to enlist in the army, and around 200,000 newly enlisted Black troops joined the fight.[16] Their contributions helped turn the tide in favor of the Union and brought the Civil War to an end.

However, because of the slow movement of information and the deliberate efforts by some to keep the news of freedom from reaching the enslaved people, many

---

[15] Schwartz, B. (2015). The Emancipation Proclamation: Lincoln's many second thoughts. *Society, 52*(6), 590–603. https://doi.org/10.1007/s12115-015-9954-7

[16] Ibid

# The U.S.'s Second Independence Day: Juneteenth

in Texas remained in bondage until June 19, 1865, when Union General Gordon Granger finally arrived in Galveston to enforce the proclamation. This day, known as Juneteenth, marks the end of slavery in the United States and serves as a reminder of the long and difficult journey to freedom.

# The U.S.'s Second Independence Day: Juneteenth

## Chapter 5: The First Juneteenth Celebrations

It has been established that Juneteenth is marked as June 19, 1865. A year later, on the same day in 1866, the first Juneteenth celebration took place[17]. This was a powerful response to the tragically delayed freedom for enslaved people in the deepest reaches of the Confederacy. Juneteenth brought Black Americans together to celebrate the memories of loved ones lost and the beginning of progress toward gaining freedom.

The early Juneteenth celebrations symbolized a new era of freedom, which eventually led to Black Americans gaining the right to vote and the ability to have due process in the eyes of the law[18]. However, these new rights were not immediately available to all, and over time, many freed Black Americans struggled under systems of oppression that favored whites.

At the first Juneteenth celebration, people came together for an open prayer, followed by parades, sporting events, and spiritually uplifting songs like "Go Down Moses" and "Many Thousands Gone."[19] In some cases, trees were set ablaze and filled with gunpowder to replace fireworks, which are commonly used today.[20]

---

[17] Scott, J. S., & Jordan, M. P. (2022, April 21-23). *Commemorative Juneteenth policies in the U.S. states: Diffusion, interests, and appeasement*. State Politics & Policy Conference. Unpublished manuscript. Available from file:///C:/Users/echoa/Downloads/625a558292c19-Juneteenth_v.1.1.%20SPPC.%20Jamil%20Scott%20&%20Marty%20Jordan,%204.23.22.pdf

[18] Moon, T. (2024, Jun 11). Pensacola Juneteenth celebrations honor the past, look to the future. *Pensacola News Journal* Retrieved from https://www.proquest.com/newspapers/pensacola-juneteenth-celebrations-honor-past-look/docview/3066194154/se-2

[19] Harris, A. (2020, June 18). *The history of Juneteenth explained*. Vox. https://www.vox.com/2020/6/18/21294825/history-of-juneteenth

[20] Idib

# The U.S.'s Second Independence Day: Juneteenth

The day's events included food, poems, and singing. These gatherings allowed the newly freed Black Americans to express pride in America's progress toward democracy.[21]

Today, across the globe, people continue to show their gratitude by joining in the celebration of freedom. Juneteenth has become a symbol for the world, recognizing the significance of freedom for everyone, not just in America but worldwide. A decade after that first Juneteenth celebration, President Rutherford B. Hayes, a newly elected Republican, encouraged the weakening of Black voting rights through gerrymandering, intimidation, and violence during the Reconstruction era (1863–1890).[22] Over time, white supremacist norms and Jim Crow laws took hold, but Juneteenth continued to offer Black Americans hope for equality.

By the 20th century, the Juneteenth celebration had spread across the country, from California to Florida. The Great Migration played a large role in this, as freed Black Americans moved to northern and western states in search of better opportunities.[23] However, Juneteenth celebrations declined during World War I and World War II, as people believed the period was too dark to be celebrated. Despite this, Juneteenth was revitalized in the 1950s and 1960s, becoming part of the civil rights movement. By 1980, Texas officially made Juneteenth a holiday, and in June 2021, President Joe Biden signed it into law as a federal holiday.[24]

---

[21] Idib
[22] Harris, A. (2020, June 18). *The history of Juneteenth explained*. Vox. https://www.vox.com/2020/6/18/21294825/history-of-juneteenth

[23] Idib
[24] Harris, A. (2020, June 18). *The history of Juneteenth explained*. Vox. https://www.vox.com/2020/6/18/21294825/history-of-juneteenth

# The U.S.'s Second Independence Day: Juneteenth

## Go Down Moses (feat. Sy Oliver Choir & The All Stars)

**Song by** Louis Armstrong

Go down, Moses,
Way down in Egypt land
Tell all Pharaohs to let my people go!

When Israel was in Egypt's land
Let my people go
Oppressed so hard they could not stand
Let my people go

So the Lord said, Go down, Moses,
Way down in Egypt land
Tell all Pharaohs to let my people go!

So, Moses went to Egypt land
Let my people go He made old Pharaoh understand
Let my people go

Yes, the Lord said, Go down, Moses,
Way down in Egypt land
Tell all Pharaohs to let my people go!

Thus spoke the Lord, bold Moses said
Let my people go
If not, I'll smite your firstborns dead.
Let my people go

God, the Lord said,
Go down, Moses,
Way down in Egypt land
Tell old Pharaoh to let my people go!

# The U.S.'s Second Independence Day: Juneteenth

Way down in Egypt land
Tell old Pharaoh to let my people go![25]

## Many Thousand Gone by Jubilee Singers

No more auction block for me
No more, no more
No more auction block for me
Many thousand gone

No more peck o' for me
No more, no more
No more peck o' corn for me
Many thousand gone

No more driver's lash for me
No more, no more
No more driver's lash for me
Many thousand gone

No more pint o' salt for me
No more, no more
No more pint o' salt for me
Many thousand gone

No more hundred lash for me
No more, no more
No more hundred lash for me
Many thousand gone

No more mistress call for me
No more, no more
No more mistress call for me

---

[25] Singing Bell. (2022). *Go down, Moses [PDF]*. Singing Bell. https://www.singing-bell.com/wp-content/uploads/2022/03/Go-Down-Moses-Lyrics-Singing-Bell.pdf

# The U.S.'s Second Independence Day: Juneteenth

Many thousand gone[26]

---

[26] Teaching American History. (n.d.). *Many thousand gone*. Teaching American History. https://teachingamericanhistory.org/document/many-thousand-gone/

# The U.S.'s Second Independence Day: Juneteenth

## Chapter 6: Juneteenth Traditions

When you attend any of today's Juneteenth celebrations, you're bound to experience the holiday's rich history embraced by those who understand its significance. In places like Pensacola, Florida, several events lead up to the main day, all bringing participants together in unity to honor the liberation of our enslaved ancestors.

These celebrations often feature vendor fairs that provide educational materials on Juneteenth, health screenings, cultural attire, and the musical sounds of freedom echoing through the air. The excitement and laughter of the day fill the atmosphere with joy.

Numerous authors set up underneath canopy tents, eager to share educational materials that enrich the minds of those eager to learn the limited, often untold, truthful stories of our past. This information is valuable to our way of life, and soaking in as much knowledge as possible is encouraged. Ceremonies are held with poetry readings, and dance performances by both the young and elderly, expressing the spirit of freedom.

The festivities serve as a bridge connecting generations, ensuring that the history and significance of Juneteenth are passed down. These events often encourage voter registration, support entrepreneurship, and continue traditional celebrations through block parties and community center activities. Fireworks light up the sky as the day's celebrations close, whether in ballparks, community centers, backyard cookouts, or church parking lots.

During election years, Juneteenth provides a unique

# The U.S.'s Second Independence Day: Juneteenth

opportunity for voters to engage with local and state representatives, discussing community concerns and addressing social disparities. Many speeches focus on the atrocities of the past and how we can build a better future for the generations to come.

Of course, no celebration is complete without food. Juneteenth gatherings bring people together to enjoy delicious dishes like barbecue, oxtails, strawberries, watermelon, red velvet cake, and red beans and rice. The presence of red foods is particularly significant, symbolizing the bloodshed during the horrors of captivity—from the African and Caribbean seashores, through the brutal Transatlantic slave trade, to the inhumane cell block sales of human beings and the painful separation of families.[27]

The resilience of those who endured bondage is honored in every bite, and the traditions of Juneteenth continue to strengthen the bonds within our communities, ensuring that the legacy of freedom and equality is celebrated and preserved.

---

[27] McDaniel, T. (2021, June 18). *Juneteenth foods and traditions explained*. History. https://www.history.com/news/juneteenth-foods-traditions

# The U.S.'s Second Independence Day: Juneteenth

## Chapter 7: The Evolution of Juneteenth

It took 156 years for Juneteenth to be recognized as a national federal holiday, making it the first new federal holiday since Dr. Martin Luther King Jr. Day was established in 1983. Although Black Texans began celebrating Juneteenth in 1866, marking their contribution to freedom, the government was slow to officially acknowledge this important day.

Even after the Emancipation Proclamation was enacted in 1863, forced slavery continued in Galveston, Texas. It wasn't until the end of the Civil War in 1865 when enough Union troops were available to enforce the law that the enslaved people in Texas were finally freed.

Fast forward to a different period of unrest in 2020, when the world witnessed the tragic killing of George Floyd by a police officer in Minnesota. This injustice, captured on video, sparked global protests and reignited conversations about systemic racism in America. In response, Bipartisan support emerged to make Juneteenth a federal holiday.

Senator Edward Markey, a Democrat from Massachusetts, spearheaded the effort, working with members of the House of Representatives and Congress to pass the Juneteenth National Independence Day Act.[28] The bill was signed into law, finally giving Juneteenth the national recognition it deserved.

---

[28] Face2Face Africa. (n.d.). *6 influential figures in the Juneteenth movement you need to know*. Face2Face Africa. https://face2faceafrica.com/article/6-influential-figures-in-the-juneteenth-movement-you-need-to-know.

# The U.S.'s Second Independence Day: Juneteenth

Since its establishment as a federal holiday, many businesses have made Juneteenth a paid holiday, further acknowledging its significance. However, it is worth noting that South Dakota has yet to officially commemorate Juneteenth until 2022 being the last holdout state.[29]

The evolution of Juneteenth from a local celebration in Texas to a national holiday reflects both the progress and the ongoing challenges in America's journey toward equality and justice. While much has been achieved, the fight for true freedom and recognition continues.

---

[29] Davis, J. (2021, June 17). *Why Juneteenth, the U.S.'s second Independence Day, is a federal holiday.* Smithsonian Magazine. https://www.smithsonianmag.com/smart-news/why-juneteenth-us-second-independence-day-federal-holiday-180978015/

# The U.S.'s Second Independence Day: Juneteenth

## Chapter 8: The Importance of Juneteenth Today

Reflecting on Juneteenth is an opportunity for everyone to recognize that Black history is American history, and American history belongs to all of us. As citizens of the United States, it is crucial to understand the significance of this history, learn from past mistakes, and strive to become better versions of ourselves. While progress has been made, there is still much work to do, particularly in fostering unity across racial and political divisions.

Our youth must be educated about this history to develop a clear understanding of civil rights struggles and what society justice looks like. When families come together within their communities to support Juneteenth, it can have a profound and positive impact on the lives of everyone involved. Positive change begins with a mindset that values the importance of everyone's life and the contributions of others to our shared future.

Juneteenth offers a unique opportunity for family traditions to be passed down, instilling a sense of pride and hope in young people. It teaches them that while the past may have been bleak, progress is possible, and they can help shape a brighter future. For Black families, Juneteenth holds a deep sense of sentiment, providing an occasion to honor historical events and to promote unity and appreciation for the significance of this day.

By understanding and embracing their history, individuals can uphold the values they've learned and take pride in the contributions of those who came before them. When we reflect on the hardships Black Americans have

## The U.S.'s Second Independence Day: Juneteenth

endured, we must also marvel at the incredible odds they overcame.

Juneteenth is more than just a celebration; it is a reminder of the resilience and strength that has shaped the nation. It is a day to acknowledge the past, recognize the progress made, and commit to building a more united and equitable future for all.

### Regarding Progress and Change in the United States

As we reflect on progress, the call to remove monuments that glorify a painful and oppressive past is not just a desire to erase history but a demand for a more just and equal future. These towering statues, often dedicated to Confederate leaders, serve as constant reminders of a time when the lives of our ancestors were devalued, and their humanity was denied. The blood that runs through our veins connects us to those who were once considered only three-fifths of a person under Article I, Section 2 of the U.S. Constitution of 1787.[30] How can we move forward when the symbols of terror and oppression still loom over our cities and towns?

The persistence of these monuments is a reflection of a broader issue: the remnants of Jim Crow laws and attitudes that continue to affect Black communities today. If such laws still exist, they must be amended to reflect the direction in which society is striving—to heal from the devastations that have crippled Black families for generations. But change cannot happen without accountability. Who is policing the police when some officers act as though they are still enforcing the old ways

---

[30] U.S. Const. art. I, § 2.

# The U.S.'s Second Independence Day: Juneteenth

of the Wild West? The law enforcement system has its share of bad actors, individuals who disregard the value of Black and Brown lives. It is unacceptable for these corrupt officers to continue their careers unchecked. Real change must begin at the top, with leadership that is committed to removing those who fail to serve and protect.

True progress also requires representation. We need more voices from local, state, and federal governments that truly understand the challenges faced by marginalized communities. Decision-makers who shape our laws and policies must have a deep, lived understanding of the struggles we endure. It is not enough to make decisions from a place of privilege—those in power must walk in our shoes, feel our pain, and share our experiences to make the right and just changes for all communities.

# The U.S.'s Second Independence Day: Juneteenth

## Chapter 9: How Children Can Celebrate Juneteenth and Learn

Juneteenth is not just a day of remembrance and celebration for adults; it's also an opportunity for children to learn about their heritage and the significance of freedom. The holiday offers a variety of family-friendly activities that allow children to embrace the legacy of resilience and triumph over racism. By participating in these activities, children can deepen their understanding of history while enjoying the spirit of celebration.

At local festivals, children are often surrounded by the musical sounds of live performances that recount stories of battles won and freedoms gained. These performances provide an engaging way for them to connect with history. Many festivals also feature creative stations where children can express their understanding of Juneteenth through art. Drawing, painting, and crafting activities centered around the themes of freedom and equality give children a chance to explore their creativity while learning about the past.

Across the United States, many communities host open houses at African American museums, where families can explore exhibits that highlight the contributions and lives of their ancestors. These visits provide a rich educational experience, helping children understand the historical context of Juneteenth and the ongoing struggle for equality.

Parades are another highlight of Juneteenth celebrations, offering children the chance to join in the joyous atmosphere, cheering and playing alongside their peers. The collective energy of these parades fosters a sense of community and shared history, making the celebration both fun and meaningful.

For many families, Juneteenth is also a time to engage in deeper conversations about the holiday's significance. Grandparents and parents can take this opportunity to explain the meaning of Juneteenth, sharing stories of pride and perseverance. These

# The U.S.'s Second Independence Day: Juneteenth

discussions encourage children to ask questions and reflect on the importance of freedom and equality, helping to instill a strong sense of cultural identity.

Other traditional Juneteenth activities include poetry readings, interpretive dance performances, and plays that bring history to life. These cultural expressions not only entertain but also educate giving children the more immersive experience of the holiday's themes.

Food is an integral part of Juneteenth celebrations, and children often look forward to tasting the various, red-themed dishes that honor the memory of those who fought and died for freedom. Red is symbolic of the bloodshed during the liberation struggle, and the sight of red velvet cakes, watermelon, and red beans and rice serves as a reminder of the sacrifices made.[31]

Some Juneteenth festivals also feature fashion and hair shows, which celebrate cultural identity and heritage. These events allow children to see beauty and pride in their culture, inspiring them to embrace their uniqueness.

Local authors who write about Juneteenth and related topics are often invited to share their work at these festivals. By listening to authors read excerpts from their books, children can gain a deeper understanding of history and be inspired to explore writing themselves. Seeing authors who look like them can be especially motivating, encouraging young readers to believe in their potential to tell stories and make a difference.

The inspiration that children gain from participating in Juneteenth celebrations can have a lasting impact, shaping their understanding of history and their role in the ongoing fight for equality. By passing down these traditions, we ensure that the legacy

---

[31] McDaniel, T. (2021, June 18). *Juneteenth foods and traditions explained.* History. https://www.history.com/news/juneteenth-foods-traditions.

## The U.S.'s Second Independence Day: Juneteenth

of Juneteenth continues to resonate with future generations. Youth need to understand Juneteenth and all that it stands for, they will be aware and better equipped for what is happening in the cities and towns.[32] The Juneteenth events have an abundance of opportunities that encourage the youth to have a sense of self-determination to apply what they have gained from one year to the next.

---

[32] Juneteenth offers new ways to teach about slavery, black perseverance, and American history (2024). Pittsburgh: Real Times, Inc. Retrieved from https://www.proquest.com/blogs-podcasts-websites/juneteenth-offers-new-ways-teach-about-slavery/docview/3075481170/se-2.

# The U.S.'s Second Independence Day: Juneteenth

## Chapter 10: A Message of Hope and Unity

Juneteenth stands as a powerful reflection of unity and the strides we've made toward progress, particularly for Black Americans, but also for all who value justice and equality.[33] The recognition of Juneteenth as a National Federal Holiday marks a milestone in our history, a victory achieved through the tireless efforts of dedicated individuals and activists.[34]

We owe much to the leaders who championed this cause, ensuring that Juneteenth's importance was recognized at the highest levels. Among them, President Joe Biden played a pivotal role in signing the bill that officially made Juneteenth a Federal Holiday on June 17, 2021. This achievement would not have been possible without the advocacy of many, including figures like H. J. Res, Barbara-Rose Collins, Lula Briggs Galloway, and the late great Sheila Jackson Lee, who sadly passed away on July 19, 2024.

A special acknowledgment goes to Opal Lee, known as the "Grandmother of Juneteenth," whose relentless activism was instrumental in making this holiday a reality.[35] Her presence beside President Biden as he signed the Juneteenth bill into law was a moment of triumph, not just for her, but for all who have fought for recognition and justice.

The message that Juneteenth conveys is clear: history must be told truthfully and fully. The past was marked by cruelty and hardship, and we owe it to ourselves and future generations to confront that reality, not to erase or sanitize it. The story of Juneteenth is one of resilience, sacrifice, and the unyielding pursuit of freedom and equality. It is a story that belongs to all of us.

---

[33] Newsworthy Women. (n.d.). *Juneteenth and its impact on Black women's rights.* https://www.msn.com/en-us/news/us/juneteenth-and-its-impact-on-black-womens-rights/ar-BB1plN1Z..
[34] iMDB
[35] Kindelan, K. (2024, June 19). *Opal Lee walked from Texas to D.C. to bring attention to Juneteenth.* ABC News. https://abcnews.go.com/GMA/News/meet-opal-lee-grandmother-movement-make-juneteenth-federal/story?id=78356537.

# The U.S.'s Second Independence Day: Juneteenth

As we look to the future, we must remember that the fight against injustice and the quest for equality is far from over. Juneteenth is a time to celebrate our cultural diversity and recommit ourselves to the remaining work. The road ahead may be long and challenging, but together, with hope and unity, we can continue to build a more just and inclusive society.

Let Juneteenth be a reminder that progress is possible and that we can achieve a better future for all through collective effort.

# The U.S.'s Second Independence Day: Juneteenth

## Chapter 11: The Juneteenth Flag

In 1997, Ben Haith, founder of the National Juneteenth Celebration Foundation (NJCF), designed the Juneteenth flag, one of the most beautiful and meaningful symbols of the holiday.[36] The flag was revised in 2000, incorporating the rich colors of red, white, and blue, which mirror those of the American flag, emphasizing that enslaved Black Americans and their descendants are American.

At the heart of the flag is a five-pointed star, symbolizing freedom for all African Americans across the United States. The red color represents the blood shed by enslaved Black Americans in their struggle for freedom. The starburst surrounding the star reflects a new beginning, and the arc in the middle of the flag symbolizes the horizon, representing the opportunities and bright future that await Black Americans.

Since its creation, the Juneteenth flag has been flown on June 19th each year, celebrating Juneteenth across different states. The flag is a powerful reminder of the resilience and hope of Black Americans and their ongoing journey toward equality and freedom.

---

[36] Philippe, McKenzie Jean. "The Juneteenth flag was created in 1997". Oprah. Archived from the original on 21 May 2022. Retrieved 27 May 2022.

# The U.S.'s Second Independence Day: Juneteenth




# The U.S.'s Second Independence Day: Juneteenth

# The U.S.'s Second Independence Day: Juneteenth

## Chapter 12: The Role of Education in Preserving Juneteenth's Legacy

Preserving the legacy of Juneteenth through education is essential for ensuring that future generations understand its powerful impact and significance. Juneteenth, which commemorates the day enslaved African Americans in Texas were finally informed of their freedom, is a pivotal moment in American history. However, its roots trace back to the broader context of the Emancipation Proclamation and the eventual abolition of slavery in the United States.

The Emancipation Proclamation, enacted by President Abraham Lincoln in 1863, initially freed enslaved African Americans in Confederate states such as Alabama, Arkansas, Florida, Georgia, Louisiana, Mississippi, North Carolina, South Carolina, Tennessee, Texas, and Virginia. These states had seceded from the Union during the Civil War, forming their government. Despite the proclamation, it wasn't until the 13th Amendment was ratified in 1865 that slavery was officially abolished throughout the United States. This historical journey is crucial for understanding why Juneteenth is more than just a day of celebration—it is a testament to the enduring struggle for freedom and equality.

Education plays a critical role in passing down the true nature of Juneteenth so that each generation does not forget the sacrifices made by our ancestors. Teaching the history and significance of Juneteenth ensures that it becomes a part of our collective consciousness, not just an annual event but a deep-seated tradition. One way to begin this education is through the powerful song "Lift Every Voice and Sing," often referred to as the Black National Anthem.[37] This song, with its themes of equity, freedom, and justice, serves as a reminder of the ongoing struggle for civil rights and should be a staple in households, schools, and churches.

---

[37] S.E. William (2022, April 23) Freedom Day And The Unfinished Symphony. chrome-extension://efaidnbmnnnibpcajpcglclefindmkaj/https://scholarworks.lib.csusb.edu/cgi/viewcontent.cgi?article=1770&context=blackvoice.

# The U.S.'s Second Independence Day: Juneteenth

As Dr. Daina Ramey Berry has pointed out, much work still needs to be done. Inclusion efforts must continue, outdated laws need revision, and freedoms must be safeguarded. Juneteenth is not just a moment to reflect on the past; it is a call to action.[38] As Dr. Kevin Cokley noted in 2022, when someone asks, "What is Juneteenth?" The response should inspire agitation, celebration, and education. The more Juneteenth is celebrated and understood, the less likely we are to overlook the profound contributions it has made to our lives.[39]

The cultural significance of Juneteenth extends beyond celebration; it fosters emotional connections, reinforces personal and cultural identity, and promotes community unity. By participating in the Juneteenth festivities, people from different backgrounds can engage with the rich experiences and traditions that the holiday supports. This engagement bridges gaps between communities, fostering a sense of shared purpose and understanding.

Through education, Juneteenth becomes more than a historical footnote—it becomes a living tradition that continues to evolve and inspire. As we teach and learn about this crucial chapter in American history, we strengthen the foundation for future generations to build upon, ensuring that the legacy of Juneteenth endures.

---

[38] Past, N. E. (2022). Resources for Understanding and Celebrating Juneteenth. chrome-extension://efaidnbmnnnibpcajpcglclefindmkaj/https://repositories.lib.utexas.edu/server/api/core/bitstreams/c8e1521d-4a59-48c6-a3dd-971983aee3b1/content.

[39] Past, N. E. (2022). Resources for Understanding and Celebrating Juneteenth. chrome-extension://efaidnbmnnnibpcajpcglclefindmkaj/https://repositories.lib.utexas.edu/server/api/core/bitstreams/c8e1521d-4a59-48c6-a3dd-971983aee3b1/content.

# The U.S.'s Second Independence Day: Juneteenth

## Chapter 13: Juneteenth and the Arts

Art plays a crucial role in connecting people to the meaning of Juneteenth. Through various forms of artistic expression, individuals have the opportunity to celebrate, express, and display African American culture from their unique perspectives. Juneteenth offers a platform for creativity, allowing people to engage with the holiday in ways that resonate with them personally and culturally.

Music is often at the heart of Juneteenth celebrations. Songs like "A Change Is Gonna Come" and "Lift Every Voice and Sing" are powerful anthems that capture the essence of the struggle for freedom and the hope for a better future. These songs, when performed during Juneteenth events, evoke a deep emotional connection to the holiday's significance.

James Weldon Johnson's **"Lift Every Voice and Sing"** Lyrics

Lift every voice and sing,
Till earth and heaven ring,
Ring with the harmonies of Liberty,
Let our rejoicing rise
High as the listening skies,
Let it resound as loud as the rolling sea.
Sing a song full of the faith that the dark past has taught us
Sing a song full of the hope that the present has brought us
Facing the rising sun of our new day,
Let us march on till victory is won.

Stony the road we trod
Bitter the chastening rod,
Felt in the days when hope unborn had died;
Yet with a steady beat
Have not our weary feet
Come to the place for which our fathers sighed?
We have come over a way that with tears has been watered
We have come, treading our path through the blood of the

# The U.S.'s Second Independence Day: Juneteenth

slaughtered.
Out from the gloomy past, till now we stand at last
Where the white gleam of our bright star is cast.

God of our weary years,
God of our silent tears,
Thou who hast brought us thus far on the way;
Thou who hast by Thy might,
Led us into the light, Keep us forever in the path, we pray.
Lest our feet stray from the places, our God, where we meet Thee,
Lest our hearts, drunk with the wine of the world we forget Thee;
Shadowed beneath Thy hand, may we forever stand,
True to our God, true to our native land.[40]

    Dance is another popular form of artistic expression during Juneteenth. Whether through traditional African dances, contemporary performances, or even spontaneous movements during parades, dance allows people to physically embody the joy and resilience that Juneteenth represents. Poetry readings also offer a way to share stories, reflections, and emotions, adding a layer of introspection to the celebrations.

    In many communities, the sounds of African drums, live music performances, and the beats from local DJs fill the air, creating a vibrant and festive atmosphere. These musical elements not only entertain but also serve as a reminder of the rich cultural heritage that Juneteenth honors.

    Comedy, too, finds its place in Juneteenth celebrations. Comedy shows bring laughter, offering a moment of escape and a way to cope with the struggles that many still face. Humor has long been a tool for resilience in the African American community, and Juneteenth provides an opportunity to celebrate this aspect of the culture.

---

[40] Johnson, J. W. (n.d.). *Lift every voice and sing [Annotated]*. Genius. https://genius.com/James-weldon-johnson-lift-every-voice-and-sing-annotated

# The U.S.'s Second Independence Day: Juneteenth

For children, Juneteenth offers a chance to engage with the arts in fun and creative ways. Face painting is a favorite activity, with designs often featuring the colors of the Juneteenth flag—red, white, and blue—or depicting favorite animals and symbols of freedom. These artistic expressions help instill a sense of pride and connection to the holiday from a young age.

Art in all its forms—whether music, dance, poetry, comedy, or visual art—helps to bring Juneteenth to life. It creates a shared experience that not only celebrates African American culture but also fosters a deeper understanding of the holiday's significance. Through the arts, Juneteenth becomes more than just a day of remembrance; it becomes a living, breathing celebration of freedom, creativity, and community.

# The U.S.'s Second Independence Day: Juneteenth

## Chapter 14: Future of Juneteenth

In recent years, Juneteenth has gained widespread popularity, not only in the United States but also in communities around the world. While the celebration of Juneteenth in the U.S. traditionally occurs on June 19th, other parts of the world observe similar holidays on different dates. For instance, the end of British colonial rule and the emancipation of enslaved people in Canada and the Caribbean were recognized on August 1, 1834. In other places, Juneteenth was celebrated on January 1, 1808, July 5th, and August 1, giving freed black people the opportunity to celebrate in open public spaces.[41]

The future of Juneteenth shines brighter than ever before. As more people learn about the holiday's significance, they increasingly embrace it through education and active participation. Juneteenth has become a symbol of freedom and resilience that resonates with people from all backgrounds. It is a day for everyone to reflect on the past, celebrate the progress made, and consider how we can continue to work toward a more just and equitable future.

The journey toward freedom for enslaved people was uneven and occurred at different times across various regions. In the United States, freedom came as early as 1861 in some areas, while in others, like Kentucky, enslaved people did not experience freedom until six months after the first battle of the Civil War between Union and Confederate troops.[42] This complexity reminds us that the struggle for freedom was, and continues to be, a multifaceted journey.

As we celebrate Juneteenth, we must not only honor the past but also reflect on the present and consider how we can address current issues to build a better future. This involves looking at pressing challenges such as police reform, violence prevention, and

---

[41] Wintz, C. D., & Morehouse, M. M. Juneteenth (1000-word entry).

[42] Harris, A. (2020, June 18). *The history of Juneteenth explained.* Vox. https://www.vox.com/2020/6/18/21294825/history-of-juneteenth

# The U.S.'s Second Independence Day: Juneteenth

the need for essential services and resources in communities that face systemic disadvantages. Substance abuse, which tragically destroys lives, is one such issue that demands our attention. By bringing awareness to these problems, we can work towards creating safer, healthier communities.

Juneteenth also offers an opportunity to focus on the well-being of our youth. We must provide them with the counseling and life skills needed to cope with past and present traumas. One critical area of concern is the safety of our children in schools, particularly in light of the alarming number of school shootings that occur each year in the United States. Unlike many other countries, the U.S. continues to grapple with this issue, and it requires urgent attention.

Countless obstacles need to be addressed, and Juneteenth provides us with a moment to reflect on the changes we can make to create a better world. By recommitting ourselves to the principles of freedom, equality, and justice that Juneteenth embodies, we can work together to tackle these challenges and build a more peaceful and inclusive society for future generations.

# The U.S.'s Second Independence Day: Juneteenth

## Chapter 15: Economic Impact of Juneteenth

Juneteenth plays a critical role in supporting Black entrepreneurs, providing a wealth of opportunities to showcase their arts, crafts, artistic expressions, vocal skills, and musical talents. The holiday has become a vibrant platform for business owners to gain visibility and connect with a broader audience. For many, Juneteenth is not just a celebration of freedom but also a significant economic event that fuels business growth and community engagement.

One of the key aspects of Juneteenth is the way it brings families together. Many people travel back to their hometowns to reconnect with the significance of Juneteenth that they first experienced in their childhood. This homecoming creates a demand for accommodation, making Bed and Breakfast establishments particularly important during this time. These businesses not only cater to visitors but also contribute to the local economy by providing a comfortable and welcoming environment for those returning to celebrate.

Black-owned businesses are at the heart of Juneteenth celebrations, showcasing the richness and diversity of the Black community. Black-owned restaurants, for example, take pride in presenting the rich flavors and culinary traditions that have been passed down through generations. Vendors work tirelessly, often putting in sleepless hours, to offer products that reflect their passion and creativity, and customers eagerly support these businesses by purchasing items that resonate with their values and tastes.

In 2024, cities like Green Bay commemorated their 5th annual Juneteenth celebration with an event called "We All Rise," which highlighted the significant contributions of Black men to their communities.[43] This celebration helped to break down societal stereotypes and uplift the positive impact that Black men have on society. Events like these not only honor cultural heritage but also

---

[43] WBAY. (2024, June 14). *We All Rise organization's Juneteenth celebration marks 5th year*. WBAY. https://www.wbay.com/2024/06/14/we-all-rise-organizations-juneteenth-celebration-marks-5th-year/

## The U.S.'s Second Independence Day: Juneteenth

create economic opportunities by attracting visitors and supporting local businesses.

For Black-owned businesses, Juneteenth represents a chance to make the most of every opportunity, fostering connections and building networks that can lead to long-term success. Business owners spend quality time with one another, sharing experiences about what has worked in their areas and what hasn't. This exchange of ideas and strategies is invaluable for entrepreneurs looking to grow and sustain their businesses.

Juneteenth also provides a unique opportunity for Black business owners to engage with local government officials, such as city council members and commissioners. These interactions allow business owners to address concerns that may be hindering their success and to advocate for policies that support economic growth within their communities.

The rise of social media has further amplified the economic impact of Juneteenth, with more people learning about pop-up events and Juneteenth celebrations that highlight the work of Black-owned businesses. This increased visibility helps to close the wealth gap, one purchase at a time, and ensures that these businesses can continue to thrive, even in challenging economic times.

However, the economic success of Juneteenth is not just about financial gain. Black business leaders understand the importance of honoring the sacrifices made by their ancestors. They pay tribute to those who fought for freedom and equality, ensuring that the spirit of Juneteenth remains alive in every transaction and every celebration.

# The U.S.'s Second Independence Day: Juneteenth

## Chapter 16: Juneteenth in the Global Context

Juneteenth is significant in the United States and offers an opportunity for reflection and action against racism worldwide. In countries across the globe, Juneteenth serves as a catalyst for confronting systemic racism within cities, townships, countryside, suburbs, and commonwealths. Racism has been a persistent issue in many nations, and Juneteenth opens the door to beginning the healing process, addressing both systemic racism and the intolerance rooted in human hearts and actions.

Systemic racism is not confined to one country; it has become a global issue. We see efforts to restrict voter rights for people of color, an increase in Anti-Asian violence, and a rise in Islamophobic attacks, particularly in Europe.[44] These challenges highlight the urgent need for global solidarity in combating racism and promoting equality. Juneteenth provides a framework for initiating these conversations and fostering change, not just in America but worldwide.

Juneteenth is primarily celebrated in the United States, where it originated. The holiday marks the emancipation of enslaved African Americans and specifically commemorates June 19, 1865, when Union soldiers arrived in Galveston, Texas, to enforce the Emancipation Proclamation, freeing the last remaining enslaved people in the Confederacy.

However, the significance of Juneteenth has reached other parts of the world, particularly among African diaspora communities. In some countries, Juneteenth is observed by expatriate communities, cultural organizations, and social justice groups, though it is not an official holiday.

For instance:

---

[27] *Why Juneteenth matters everywhere in the world.* (2022, June). World Economic Forum. https://www.weforum.org/agenda/2022/06/why-juneteenth-matters-everywhere/.

# The U.S.'s Second Independence Day: Juneteenth

**Canada**: Some cities with large African Canadian populations, such as Toronto, hold Juneteenth events, often in conjunction with celebrations of Emancipation Day, which marks the abolition of slavery in the British Empire.

**United Kingdom**: Juneteenth events are also held by African and Caribbean communities in the UK, focusing on the broader themes of freedom, human rights, and the African American struggle.

**Other Countries**: In places like Mexico, Ghana, and other parts of Africa, there may be smaller, community-driven observances of Juneteenth, often organized by African American expatriates or those interested in African American history and culture.

While Juneteenth's recognition is growing internationally, it is still most widely and officially celebrated within the United States. Juneteenth is a great way for familiar faces and non-familiar faces to support black-owned businesses and the festivals and all hard work to bring insight into recognizing how far we have come. Each community around the world has so much to offer and not one person knows everything. This opportunity of Juneteenth helps black-owned businesses obtain in-depth insight into what is happening where they live. But it also helps us understand that other countries have the same struggles, and we could educate ourselves on the fight for global equity for all.[45]

---

[45] Time. (n.d.). *This Juneteenth, Black America has an important opportunity to increase its global impact*. Time. http://time.com/618693/juneteenth-black-american-blm-global-impact/

# The U.S.'s Second Independence Day: Juneteenth

## Chapter 17: Juneteenth in Popular Culture

Juneteenth's integration into popular culture can be a powerful tool for education and awareness. However, the persistence of hidden and overt racism in mass media continues to be a significant challenge. For instance, racist imagery has appeared in advertisements in China, and television shows in Australia have featured actors in blackface—both stark reminders that prejudice remains embedded in popular culture.[46]

In 2021, during a Europa League football game, a player from the Czech Republic shouted a racial slur at an opposing player, calling him a "monkey."[47] The next day, fans from the same team took to social media to hurl the n-word at the player. The situation escalated as fans continued to make monkey chants during subsequent games. These incidents are painful reminders that racism, fueled by ignorance and hate, is still prevalent in various forms of popular culture around the world.

Juneteenth provides a crucial opportunity to educate and bring awareness to these issues. Despite its growing recognition, many people worldwide remain unaware of Juneteenth and its significance. One way to combat this lack of awareness is through initiatives like the University of Maryland Global Campus (UMGC), which hosted a Juneteenth Europe Book Club event at Ramstein Air Base. This event, part of their diversity, equality, and inclusion program, featured recorded videos from faculty in Asia and Europe, educating the community about Juneteenth and fostering a global dialogue.[48]

---

[46] Why Juneteenth matters everywhere in the world. (2022, June). World Economic Forum. https://www.weforum.org/agenda/2022/06/why-juneteenth-matter-everywhere/.

[47] Euronews. (2021, March 25). *Has a football scandal exposed endemic racism in the Czech Republic?* https://www.euronews.com/my-europe/2021/03/25/has-a-football-scandal-exposed-endemic-racism-in-the-czech-republic

[48] *Juneteenth: Carrying its meaning around the world.* (2022, June). UMGC News. http://www.umgc.edu/news/archives/2022/06/juneteenth-carrying-its-meaning-around-the-world

# The U.S.'s Second Independence Day: Juneteenth

## Chapter 18: Juneteenth and Political Activism

Ms. Opal Lee, known as the "Grandmother of Juneteenth," played a pivotal role in the journey to make June 19th a federal holiday.[49] Her tireless efforts, which included walking for two and a half years from her home to the U.S. Capitol, were driven by her commitment to ensuring that the significance of Juneteenth was recognized at the national level.[50] This journey, which took her four months to complete in 2016, symbolized her dedication to the cause and her belief in the power of grassroots activism. Thanks to her persistent advocacy, Juneteenth was finally established as a national holiday in 2021, making it the first new federal holiday since President Ronald Reagan signed Dr. Martin Luther King Jr. Day into law in 1983.

Ms. Opal Lee's activism is a powerful example of how individual efforts can lead to monumental change. Her work not only brought Juneteenth to national attention but also inspired a new wave of political empowerment, particularly among Black women.[51] The fight for civil rights, including the right to vote and suffrage, has deep roots in the struggles of the 1950s and 1960s, especially in the South. Even today, the battle to protect and expand voting rights continues, reflecting the ongoing relevance of the issues that Juneteenth symbolizes.

The legacy of activism surrounding Juneteenth can also be seen in the work of Reverend Jack Yates, who established the first African American church in Houston, Texas, and founded Emancipation Park.[52] This park became a central gathering place for Juneteenth celebrations in Texas, providing a space for the community to come together and honor their history. Yates' efforts

---

[49] Kindelan, K. (2024, June 19). *Opal Lee walked from Texas to D.C. to bring attention to Juneteenth*. ABC News. https://abcnews.go.com/GMA/News/meet-opal-lee-grandmother-movement-make-juneteenth-federal/story?id=78356537.

[50] Imdb.

[51] Face2Face Africa. (n.d.). *6 influential figures in the Juneteenth movement you need to know*. Face2Face Africa. https://face2faceafrica.com/article/6-influential-figures-in-the-juneteenth-movement-you-need-to-know

[52] Imdb

# The U.S.'s Second Independence Day: Juneteenth

laid the groundwork for future generations to continue the fight for freedom and equality.[53]

In more recent years, the Black Lives Matter (BLM) movement has played a significant role in amplifying the significance of Juneteenth. BLM used its platform to advocate for national recognition of the holiday while simultaneously fighting for equality and justice. The movement's focus on addressing systemic racism and police brutality aligns closely with the struggles that Juneteenth represents. By connecting the past with the present, BLM has helped to ensure that Juneteenth remains a vital part of the ongoing fight for civil rights in America.[54]

Juneteenth's journey from a regional celebration to a federally recognized holiday is a testament to the power of political activism. It shows how sustained efforts—whether through the determined steps of Ms. Opal Lee or the collective voices of movements like BLM—can lead to lasting change. As we continue to celebrate Juneteenth, it's important to remember that the fight for freedom and equality is ongoing and that political activism remains a crucial tool in this struggle.

---

[53] Face2Face Africa. (n.d.). *6 influential figures in the Juneteenth movement you need to know*. Face2Face Africa. https://face2faceafrica.com/article/6-influential-figures-in-the-juneteenth-movement-you-need-to-know
[54] Imdb

# The U.S.'s Second Independence Day: Juneteenth

## Chapter 19: Juneteenth and the Church

As Juneteenth has grown in popularity, churches have embraced the holiday as a meaningful opportunity to bring their congregations and communities together. Local churches have integrated Juneteenth celebrations into their life centers, parking lots, and even their pulpits, extending their reach to people who might not regularly attend church services. By thinking outside the box, churches have found multiple ways to support Juneteenth in ways that are inclusive and free to the public, welcoming people from all walks of life.

One of the key elements of these church-led Juneteenth celebrations is the focus on community and spiritual growth. Many events begin with a prayer breakfast, where participants give thanks to Our Lord and Savior for His blessings in their lives. This sets a tone of gratitude and reflection for the day's activities.

Churches often incorporate a variety of activities into their Juneteenth celebrations, catering to a wide range of interests. For instance, 5K runs and walks are commonly included in the program, offering a way for participants to engage in physical activity while supporting a good cause. Praise and worship sessions, featuring singing and dancing, are also central to these celebrations, allowing attendees to express their joy and faith through music.

In addition to spiritual activities, many churches use Juneteenth as an opportunity to give back to the community. Helping hands are extended to individuals facing difficult circumstances, providing them with resources such as food, shelter, and legal assistance. On special occasions, the church might honor a prominent community member with a key to the city, recognizing their contributions and building excitement for the day. A newly drafted proclamation might be issued and read, further adding to the significance of the celebration.

# The U.S.'s Second Independence Day: Juneteenth

Juneteenth festivals organized by churches often bring a lively atmosphere filled with food trucks, vendor markets, and live musical acts, including performances by local church choirs. Poetry readings and other cultural activities add to the richness of the experience. Many participants bring lawn chairs, fans, and coolers, ready to spend the day enjoying the festivities without any rush to return to their daily challenges.

Weekend events might include performances by recording artists, outdoor movie screenings, and free admission to local museums. These activities not only entertain but also educate and inspire, fostering a sense of unity and shared purpose within the community.

Juneteenth celebrations within the church context have proven to be a powerful way to bring people together, creating a space for spiritual growth, learning, and enjoyment. Through these events, churches play a vital role in strengthening the bonds within their communities and ensuring that the legacy of Juneteenth is honored and preserved.[55]

---

[55] Unity. (n.d.). *Juneteenth and the Black church*. Unity. https://www.unity.org/en/article/juneteenth-and-black-church

# The U.S.'s Second Independence Day: Juneteenth

## Chapter 20: Juneteenth Personal Stories

## Personal Stories: Juneteenth in Belmont-DeVilliers

My experiences of Juneteenth celebrations—especially those held in the Belmont-DeVilliers neighborhood of Pensacola, Florida—are forever entwined with memories of my dear friend, Georgia Blackmon. Georgia owned the Gathering Awareness and Book Center near Belmont and DeVilliers Streets. The Gathering, as it was fondly called, was filled with books on African American history, civil rights, and inclusion. It was a welcoming place where people of all backgrounds could learn from and about each other. And the best part? You never knew who you might encounter there!

Georgia was a politically minded activist and advocate, inspiring countless people—including me—with her passion for justice and community engagement. There's no telling how many yard signs, phone lists, or campaign materials she asked me to bring her over the years. Candidates, causes—whatever it was, Georgia was involved.

Sadly, we lost Georgia in September 2023, at the age of 82. I know she would have loved to witness the historic moment when the first woman of African American and South Asian descent was nominated for the office of President of the United States. As a delegate to the 2024 Democratic National Convention, I proudly wore a button with Georgia's photo on it throughout the event, honoring her memory and the legacy she left behind.

Georgia always reminded us that milestones like Juneteenth, and moments of progress in politics, matter deeply to everyone— "across race and gender," as she often said. Her words resonate now more than ever: *We are not going back.*

#WeAreNotGoingBack
— *Jeff Nall*

# The U.S.'s Second Independence Day: Juneteenth

## Personal Stories: Juneteenth

Growing up in the 1950s, I had never heard of Juneteenth. Back then, thanks to Carter G. Woodson, we observed Negro History Week, which gave us a glimpse into our heritage—but there was so much more that we didn't know.

For many years, our celebrations revolved around the Fourth of July, with no mention of Juneteenth. It wasn't until recently that I learned about Juneteenth, and the experience has been incredible. Celebrating Juneteenth *before* the Fourth of July feels transformative. It's "coming together" in unity for everyone involved, allowing us to share in the joy and significance of the holiday.

It feels like, at last, our existence is acknowledged in history—and now, everybody knows!

– Ardelia Wilson

## Personal Juneteenth Experiences and Thoughts

What is Juneteenth to the African American? As I reflect on my ancestry and everything they endured, I think of my great-great-grandmother. She was just 8 years old when she was separated from her parents and sold off the coast of South Carolina. Juneteenth, celebrated in 1865, signifies joy—knowing that freedom eventually came. Yet, that freedom came late for the people of Texas, more than a year after the Emancipation Proclamation, and it was not without cost.

To be honest, it was only a few years ago that I started learning about Juneteenth. This part of history was not included in the schoolbooks I read during middle school and high school. Now, I

# The U.S.'s Second Independence Day: Juneteenth

am filled with a sense of pride seeing how communities come together each year to celebrate it.

    Juneteenth is personal for many of us. It gives us a sense of belonging and ownership over a part of history that was long overlooked. Learning from the past is not just about remembering, it is also about moving forward into the future with purpose and understanding.

— *Edna Rivers*


## Juneteenth on the Gulf Coast

Since the tragic loss of George Floyd during the COVID-19 years, Juneteenth has become even more prominent, especially in Pensacola, Florida. As the world renewed its focus on celebrating Juneteenth, I became curious and eager to learn more about the holiday. I took it upon myself to educate my employers about Juneteenth and advocated for it to be recognized as a paid holiday. After it became an official federal holiday, I thought, *wow, this is a step forward—things are changing.*

However, I was later disappointed to see that Juneteenth wasn't added to the official company holiday schedule. Instead, they offered a virtual chapel on Juneteenth, which was a meaningful hour filled with insightful and refreshing information. The following year, I was informed that if I wanted to celebrate Juneteenth, I'd need to use a personal holiday day from my yearly vacation benefits. And so, for the past few years, I've made it a point to save my holiday for June 19th to ensure I could celebrate this meaningful day.

Having the opportunity to experience Juneteenth in person has been nothing short of exhilarating. In my first year, I attended the celebration as a black business owner, having just launched a T-shirt company. In the following years, I decided to participate as an

# The U.S.'s Second Independence Day: Juneteenth

attendee and found it to be one of the most euphoric experiences of my life. Being immersed in the joy, seeing smiles on everyone's faces, hearing laughter in the air, and listening to soulful spiritual music filled my heart.

In Pensacola, the Juneteenth celebrations span several days leading up to June 19th. From early morning activities to late-night fireworks at Wahoo Stadium, the city is alive with events indoors and outdoors throughout the downtown area. These celebrations are vibrant, joyful, and carefully organized to ensure a safe, inclusive, and enriching experience for everyone. The sense of unity and community spirit that flows through these events has left me with cherished memories and a deep appreciation for this special holiday.

– *Dr. Mike Eric Martin*

# The U.S.'s Second Independence Day: Juneteenth

## Chapter 21: In Closing

In conclusion, Juneteenth is celebrated around the world and has led to significant strides in the fight for equality, hope, justice, and unity for all individuals. While the Emancipation Proclamation helped start the process of ending slavery, other key moments in history contributed to this progress, including the passage of the 13th Amendment two months after the end of the Civil War. Bills and legal measures had to be passed to ensure that all Americans could experience the progress represented by Juneteenth, which eventually became the 12th national federal holiday.

The resilience of activists like Opal Lee, who fought tirelessly for recognition, has allowed us to enjoy the liberties that come with being free to celebrate and learn about Juneteenth. Throughout its history, Juneteenth has seen periods of both decline and revival, with the most recent resurgence following the tragic killing of George Floyd by police officers in 2020. This event reignited the conversation around racial justice in America and gave new significance to the celebration of Juneteenth.

Americans who left Texas and traveled around the country brought Juneteenth with them, helping to spread knowledge of the holiday and its importance. While Juneteenth is now celebrated on June 19th, there were other dates throughout history on which emancipation was celebrated, such as January 1st, May 8th, July 5th, and August 1st.[56] In different states, the process of abolishing slavery looked different, and freedom was celebrated at various points in time. It's also important to remember that while America celebrated its independence on the Fourth of July, it took another 89 years for slavery to officially end.

If we fail to teach our children about Juneteenth and other critical historical moments, future generations will be at risk of losing the progress that has been made. As of 2021, upwards of 44

---

[56] Wintz, C. D., & Morehouse, M. M. Juneteenth (1000-word entry).

## The U.S.'s Second Independence Day: Juneteenth

states have made efforts to restrict discussions of critical race theory, racism, and sexism in public schools.[57] We must continue to pass on the lessons of Juneteenth and fight against attempts to erase this vital history.

I will never stop believing that the United States must apologize for its original sin of supporting and embracing slavery for financial gain. This practice caused profound harm, and its effects continue to reverberate throughout society today. Although slavery represented the worst of humanity, its replacement—*involuntary servitude through the prison system*—has proven to rival and, in some ways, surpass the inhuman treatment endured by enslaved people over the years.[58]

---

[57] Davis, J. (2021, June 17). *Why Juneteenth, the U.S.'s second Independence Day, is a federal holiday.* Smithsonian Magazine. https://www.smithsonianmag.com/smart-news/why-juneteenth-us-second-independence-day-federal-holiday-180978015/

[58] Ross, A., Bardelli, T., & Aiyuba, T. (2024, June 19). End legal slavery in the United States: Guest essay. *New York Times (Online).* https://www.proquest.com/docview/3069444120?accountid=206742&sourcetype=Blogs,%20Podcasts,%20&%20Websites

# The U.S.'s Second Independence Day: Juneteenth

## Chapter 22: Glossary

- **Ancestors** – A person from whom one is descended and who lived several generations ago.
- **Civil War** – A war within one country between different groups or regions of that country.
- **Confederate** – About the eleven southern states that separated from the United States in 1860-1861.
- **Democracy** – A form of government in which power rests with the people, either directly or through elected representatives.
- **Equality** – The condition, fact, or quality of being equal.
- **Emancipation Proclamation** – The declaration issued by President Lincoln in 1862 that freed all slaves in Confederate states not yet under Union control during the United States Civil War.
- **Enslaved** – Being without liberty and considered the property of another.
- **Entrepreneurship** – The act of assuming the financial risk of beginning and operating a business.
- **Freedom** – The condition of being free or liberated, liberty.
- **Injustice** – The lack of justice or fairness.
- **Jim Crow** – Laws and practices that enforced or promoted discrimination against or segregation of Black Americans in the United States, particularly in the South, from the late 1870s into the 1960s.
- **Juneteenth** – The anniversary and celebration of June 19, 1865, when the abolition of slavery in the Confederate states was announced in Texas by Union Army forces.
- **Liberation** – The act of freeing someone or something from oppression or captivity.
- **Marginalized Communities** – Groups of people who are excluded or treated as unimportant, often to divert attention from their needs or concerns.
- **Perseverance** – Steadfast continuance in a course of action, task, or belief despite difficulty or delay.

# The U.S.'s Second Independence Day: Juneteenth

- **Political Agenda** – A set of policies or issues to be discussed or pursued in a political context.
- **Pride** – A feeling of self-respect and worthiness.
- **Resilience** – The capacity to withstand and recover quickly from difficulties or adversity.
- **Retaliation** – The act of striking back or taking revenge.
- **Slavery** – The practice of owning people as property and holding them in bondage.
- **Social Disparities** – Conditions or instances of inequality or difference within a group or community.
- **The Union** – Refers to the northern states during the American Civil War that were opposed to the Confederate states.
- **The United States of America** – A country in North America.
- **Transatlantic Slave Trade** – The transportation of enslaved Africans across the Atlantic Ocean to the Americas for sale.
- **U.S. Constitution of 1787** – The foundational set of laws by which the United States is governed.
- **Voter Registration** – The act or process of enrolling to vote in elections.
- **White Supremacist** – A person who believes that white people are superior to those of all other races and should dominate society.
- **World War I** – A major war fought from 1914 to 1918, primarily in Europe, between the Allies (including France, Great Britain, and the United States) and the Central Powers (including Germany and Austria-Hungary).
- **World War II** – A major global conflict fought from 1939 to 1945, involving the Allies (including Great Britain, the United States, and the Soviet Union) against the Axis Powers (including Germany, Italy, and Japan).

# The U.S.'s Second Independence Day: Juneteenth

## REFERENCES

The President of the United States of America. (2024). Title 3--The President: Juneteenth Day of Observance, 2024. Washington, DC: Federal Information & News Dispatch, LLC. Retrieved from ProQuest Central: https://www.proquest.com/reports/title-3-president-juneteenth-day-observance-2024/docview/3071120891/se-2.

Library of Congress. (n.d.). *Today in history - June 19*. https://www.loc.gov/item/today-in-history/june-19/.

Edrich, P. (2023, August 22). *City coming to terms with its vital role in the slave trade: Liverpool legacy's as 'capital of transatlantic slave trade' remembered in series of events for Slavery Remembrance Day*. Liverpool Echo. Available from file:///C:/Users/echoa/Downloads/At_Home_in_the_World%E2%80%9D_Materi.pdf.

Shobowale, S. (2022, August 17). *Globes shining light on the transatlantic slave trade: Artworks form a trail around the city as a reminder of our history*. Leicester Mercury, 18. https://www.proquest.com/docview/2703043768?accountid=206742&sourcetype=Newspapers.

Howard-Hassmann, R. E. (2022). Should the USA offer reparations to Africa for the transatlantic slave trade? *Society, 59*(3), 339–348. https://doi.org/10.1007/s12115-022-00682-3.

Batchis, S. (2023, July 23). *History of racism must be taught: The United States was built on slavery. Yet, in many U.S. history courses, slavery is barely discussed. Philadelphia Inquirer*, E.1. https://www.proquest.com/docview/2840737224?accountid=206742&sourcetype=Newspapers.

# The U.S.'s Second Independence Day: Juneteenth

Juneteenth offers new ways to teach about slavery, black perseverance, and American history (2024). Pittsburgh: Real Times, Inc. Retrieved from https://www.proquest.com/blogs-podcasts-websites/juneteenth-offers-new-ways-teach-about-slavery/docview/3075481170/se-2.

Schwartz, B. (2015). The Emancipation Proclamation: Lincoln's many second thoughts. *Society, 52*(6), 590–603. https://doi.org/10.1007/s12115-015-9954-7.

Scott, J. S., & Jordan, M. P. (2022, April 21-23). *Commemorative Juneteenth policies in the U.S. states: Diffusion, interests, and appeasement.* State Politics & Policy Conference. Unpublished manuscript. Available from file:///C:/Users/echoa/Downloads/625a558292c19-Juneteenth_v.1.1.%20SPPC,%20Jamil%20Scott%20&%20Marty%20Jordan,%204.23.22.pdf.

Moon, T. (2024, Jun 11). Pensacola Juneteenth celebrations honor the past, look to the future. *Pensacola News Journal* Retrieved from https://www.proquest.com/newspapers/pensacola-juneteenth-celebrations-honor-past-look/docview/3066194154/se-2.

Harris, A. (2020, June 18). *The history of Juneteenth explained.* Vox. https://www.vox.com/2020/6/18/21294825/history-of-juneteenth.

Singing Bell. (2022). *Go down, Moses [PDF].* Singing Bell. https://www.singing-bell.com/wp-content/uploads/2022/03/Go-Down-Moses-Lyrics-Singing-Bell.pdf.

Teaching American History. (n.d.). *Many thousand gone.* Teaching American History. https://teachingamericanhistory.org/document/many-thousand-gone/.

McDaniel, T. (2021, June 18). *Juneteenth foods and traditions*

# The U.S.'s Second Independence Day: Juneteenth

*explained*. History. https://www.history.com/news/juneteenth-foods-traditions.

Face2Face Africa. (n.d.). *6 influential figures in the Juneteenth movement you need to know*. Face2Face Africa. https://face2faceafrica.com/article/6-influential-figures-in-the-juneteenth-movement-you-need-to-know.

Davis, J. (2021, June 17). *Why Juneteenth, the U.S.'s second Independence Day, is a federal holiday*. Smithsonian Magazine. https://www.smithsonianmag.com/smart-news/why-juneteenth-us-second-independence-day-federal-holiday-180978015/.

U.S. Const. art. I, § 2.

Newsworthy Women. (n.d.). *Juneteenth and its impact on Black women's rights*. https://www.msn.com/en-us/news/us/juneteenth-and-its-impact-on-black-womens-rights/ar-BB1plN1Z.

Kindelan, K. (2024, June 19). *Opal Lee walked from Texas to D.C. to bring attention to Juneteenth*. ABC News. https://abcnews.go.com/GMA/News/meet-opal-lee-grandmother-movement-make-juneteenth-federal/story?id=78356537.

Philippe, McKenzie Jean. "The Juneteenth flag was created in 1997". Oprah. Archived from the original on 21 May 2022. Retrieved 27 May 2022.

S.E. William (2022, April, 23) Freedom Day And The Unfinished Symphony. chrome-extension://efaidnbmnnnibpcajpcglclefindmkaj/https://scholarworks.lib.csusb.edu/cgi/viewcontent.cgi?article=1770&context=blackvoice.

Past, N. E. (2022). Resources for Understanding and Celebrating Juneteenth.chrome-extension://efaidnbmnnnibpcajpcglclefindmkaj/https://repositories.li

# The U.S.'s Second Independence Day: Juneteenth

b.utexas.edu/server/api/core/bitstreams/c8e1521d-4a59-48c6-a3dd-971983aee3b1/content.

Wintz, C. D., & Morehouse, M. M. Juneteenth (1000-word entry).

WBAY. (2024, June 14). *We All Rise organization's Juneteenth celebration marks 5th year*. WBAY. https://www.wbay.com/2024/06/14/we-all-rise-organizations-juneteenth-celebration-marks-5th-year/.

Time. (n.d.). *This Juneteenth, Black America has an important opportunity to increase its global impact*. Time. http://time.com/618693/juneteenth-black-american-blm-global-impact/.

Why Juneteenth matters everywhere in the world. (2022, June). World Economic Forum. https:///www.weforum.org/agenda/2022/06/why-juneteenth-matter-everywhere/.

Euronews. (2021, March 25). *Has a football scandal exposed endemic racism in the Czech Republic?* https://www.euronews.com/my-europe/2021/03/25/has-a-football-scandal-exposed-endemic-racism-in-the-czech-republic.

*Juneteenth: Carrying its meaning around the world*. (2022, June). UMGC News. http://www.umgc.edu/news/archives/2022/06/juneteenth-carrying-its-meaning-around-the-world.

# The U.S.'s Second Independence Day: Juneteenth

## ABOUT THE AUTHOR

Dr. Mike Eric Martin is a native of Philadelphia, Mississippi. He spent his adult life as the founder of *A Social Butterfly Life*, a black-owned, home-based custom apparel business. With over 20 years of experience as a Florida-certified social worker, Dr. Martin has dedicated his career to serving vulnerable children and families, mental health clients, and those in foster care. He holds a doctorate in Organizational Leadership, a master's in management, and a bachelor's degree in social work.

Dr. Martin is passionate about education, reading, and empowering youth to understand that learning is the key to success. He is the author of the children's book *We Are of African Descendants* and the coloring book *The United States of America*. He completed his dissertation *Leadership Strategies To Assist In Reducing Turnover In Substance Abuse Treatment Program* at Northcentral University in 2019.

Made in the USA
Columbia, SC
14 November 2024